Fire from the Heart 2023

Winners of the 2023 Muriel's Journey Poetry Prize

THREE OCEAN PRESS

Library and Archives Canada Cataloguing in Publication

Title: Fire from the heart, 2023 : winners of the 2023 Muriel's Journey Poetry Prize.
Other titles: Winners of the 2023 Muriel's Journey Poetry Prize
Identifiers: Canadiana (print) 20230524907 | Canadiana (ebook) 20230524915 | ISBN 9781988915470 (softcover) | ISBN 9781988915487 (EPUB)
Subjects: Canadian poetry (English)—21st century. | LCSH: Canadian poetry—21st century. | LCGFT: Poetry.
Classification: LCC PS8293.1 .F578 2023 | DDC C811/.608—dc23

Editor: Kyle Hawke
Cover and Book Designer: Kyle Hawke
Cover art: *Untitled* ©2023 Yanli Tang

Three Ocean Press
8168 Riel Place
Vancouver, BC, V5S 4B3
778.321.0636
info@threeoceanpress.com
www.threeoceanpress.com

First publication, September 2023

MURIEL'S JOURNEY

Here we are, Muriel's Journey Poetry Prize #5! Let me tell you a little about "Fortuna's Choice," the randomly drawn prize. I'm so glad we came up with this idea because every single year, Fortuna has been very smart and chosen an exquisite poem. It makes me feel humble. Of course it would be impossible to pull off something like this prize without the first readers and judges — but there is a mysterious wisdom and beauty in Dame Fortuna's choices. Maybe the Muses are looking down at us with a benevolent smile.

Much gratitude to Kyle Hawke, my co-organizer, who one day, more or less last minute before our celebration five years ago said, "Hey, I'll make a chapbook!" He's been my collaborator ever since. Thanks also to our judges, Heidi Greco, Candie Tanaka, and Rosemary Georgeson. The fabulous cover art is by Yanli Tang. Our first readers this year were Sally Quon and Catherine Garrett, and Tova Mori was our administrative assistant. A big shoutout, too, to the Heart of the City Festival, the Carnegie Centre, and Word Vancouver, all three of whom are becoming close collaborators.

ISABELLA MORI, on the traditional, ancestral, and unceded territory of the Sḵwx̱wú7mesh (Squamish), Səlílwətaʔ/Selilwitulh (Tsleil-Waututh) and xʷməθkʷəy̓əm (Musqueam) Nations, (Vancouver, BC, Canada)

ABOUT MURIEL AND THE PRIZE

Muriel was a social justice activist, poet, and spoken word artist of Indigenous heritage from the Gitxsan nation's Owl Clan who spent a lot of time in the Downtown Eastside. In her work, she always explored new ways of expressing herself, always talked and wrote about what's urgent and important. Her energy was like fireworks, and her hugs legendary.

Muriel died in November of 2018. At Muriel's memorial at the DTES' Listening Post, someone related that on her last day, Muriel said that while she was leaving, she was still continuing her journey. The text was accompanied by a picture of the sunrise on the day she died. Isabella was moved by this to do her part in Muriel's continued journey and decided to start a poetry prize in Muriel's honour.

Everyone liked Muriel. She encouraged creative people of all stripes to continue on their path of creativity and social justice. With the Muriel's Journey Poetry Prize, we hope to pass on inspiration and strength to all who create with a sense of justice in mind.

Because Muriel always did things a little differently, we're doing this poetry prize differently too. Being keenly aware of how subjective the judging of poetry can be, we give a prize to a poet randomly selected from the longlist of those who met the entry requirement of "lively, outspoken ideas … speak your mind and let the world know what you think … look at your subject in an unexpected way … take a risk in your composition … be frank and unreserved." Another change is our 'entry fee', which consists of people showing how they contribute to their community. Lastly, we have two first prizes, a general one and one specifically for a poet with close ties to the Downtown Eastside.

All poems in this collection were submitted and subsequently were selected by judges as the winners of the fifth annual Muriel's Journey Poetry Prize.

Prizes were awarded at a ceremony on September 9, 2023 as part of the Word Vancouver literary arts festival. The ceremony was hosted from the traditional and unceded territory of the Musqueam, Squamish, and Tsleil-Waututh peoples, but included winners reading from their home territories, as noted in their Community Involvement statements at the end of this book.

ORGANIZERS
Isabella Mori
Kyle Hawke

JUDGES
Candie Tanaka
Heidi Greco
Rosemary Georgeson

Special thanks to the Vancouver Public Library, the Carnegie Centre, and the Heart of the City Festival for allowing us a platform to build on, as well as to Glenn Mori, who worked out the slushing system for the poems. Thanks also to Cecily Nicholson, Diane Wood, Danielle LaFrance, and past organizer Rudolf Penner, without whom this whole project would have never happened.

The Muriel's Journey Poetry Prize honours the vitality, vivacity, and outspoken presence of poet-activist Muriel Marjorie, who passed on in the fall of 2018. As an Indigenous social justice activist, poet, and spoken word artist, what Muriel had to say would often literally wake you up. Her enthusiastic encouragement of innovative creative endeavours was infectious.

The Muriel's Journey Poetry Prize is open to all residents of Canada and to Canadians living abroad. No submission fee is charged; instead, those entering are asked to provide a statement of their community involvement to demonstrate their active effort to improve the world around them. First prize is $100. The DTES prize is also $100 and celebrates poets with a deep connection to Vancouver's Downtown Eastside. Second prize is $50. Fortuna's Choice rewards one randomly selected poem with $35. Judges look for lively, outspoken texts that present ideas in unexpected ways.

For information on the Muriel's Journey Poetry Prize, please contact the organizers at poetryprize@murielsjourney.com or visit their Facebook page.

www.murielsjourney.com

Contents

adver/city
Daniela Elza

2023

Today the present tense hurts

      the police are sweeping the streets
         in a downtown tranquilized
              with neglect.

"it's your fault if you are homeless" cuts
any way you think of it.
          no matter the century.

the soul here dies   a slow death from
multiple   paper-pushing   cuts.

we toe   the poverty line
work on   reminding our city *the facts.*

but they can afford to sustain   amnesia
         on six-digit salaries
a narrative without regret.

it is not your fault you are homeless

I keep repeating to myself
       as if I too might forget.

     <>

2020   *(found poem)*

The park was mostly empty of people
when the bulldozing began. [1]

     "My son's ashes were in that tent,"
     said Kim   leaving Oppenheimer Park

     tent city.   "And my mom's.
     Everything   ended up   in a dumpster."

       *

Kim will miss this place.

     "People were always laughing
     and drinking, partying and fighting.

     We all worked together to make sure
     everyone was taken care of."

     "It was like having cable TV
     right outside your tent," she said.

Everyone had two weeks to vacate or
face arrests.

       <>

---

1   https://www.vice.com/en/article/g5ppvq/the-last-days-of-oppenheimer-park-
vancouvers-tent-city

2022

We can outlast you   says the developer
fiddle with the meaning of public space

replace history   with bafflegab[2]

we will torture you by obfuscation
stifle the commons   the sacred grounds

     turn them into condos.

we will erase you
              empty you   of memory
of heritage   in the tumbler of   endless

   orange-   cone-   construction-   zones.

     the devil is in:

1. *the details you will not have*

2. *the language of rubble you don't have*
     enough lifetimes   to wade through

3. *the consequences you'll   pay for*
     once we are done   and long gone.

               <>

over

---

2   https://thetyee.ca/Analysis/2021/12/03/Torture-By-Planning/

2023

Time is fast-forwarding
             into   *haves* and *have-nots*

the police are pushing   and shoving
           press a face into the asphalt

         get busy   handcuffing.

we spin in a deadly whirlwind
no weather channel is willing to report.

pushing and shoving   the pain
             re- shuffling a history
             too hard to face.

a face facing the asphalt   is
       too busy   facing   the asphalt.

           <>

Oppenheimer Park Move

Gilles Cyrenne

A crow eats a dead rat

     City crew shovels tents
         shopping carts   suitcases
         sleeping bags   blankets buckets
         mattresses bicycles wheels frames
         chairs cushions rugs tarps rags
         flotsam and jetsom from unhoused lives
         into dump trucks

    A woman obstructs   grabs her backpack
         from a worker
         It's handcuffs until
she settles down   the police let her go
    she agrees to be quick
     gather possessions
       from the tent   her home
     and the crew prepares to tear it down

        Ten minutes notice
        for tent city residents
     What to sort   what to pack
     What to move   what to take   what to leave
     When equipment sum total is a shopping cart
        already you basically got nothing
        After this you'll have even less

   What's next when what remains
  is a foamy   a sleeping bag
two pop crates and a couple of blankets
           on a piece of sidewalk

over

Your bedroom   bare concrete
and all you own
          clothes on your back
          and a few coins
          in a paper cup

     A rat runs into a dry hole
                    in
                         dirt
          under tree roots
                              for
          shelter from the storm

The Orange Door
Cristy Watson

we meet at the intersection of East Third and Lonsdale,
sidle across Burrard Inlet — fifteen minutes on the spurning waves
(less arduous than ship crossings in the 1880s)

slip off the main streets of West Hastings and Homer
on our quest for Saturday night revels! past Carrall, where East
meets West in the derelict and starless alleyways off
Pender, where two shadows huddle in the shadows, a
transgression between them (I'm the fifth wheel
in our evening shenanigans) to the Orange Door, which is
just that.

we knit brown bags into crooks in our arms, blink in the gloom;
stashed bottles of rum and vodka like it's 1905 and the saloons
are being shut down again.

spot two policemen at a table near the back of the room;
finished with their plates, they nod our way, tip their
caps, and the server, before heading back onto the paths of night —
their purview; *transgressions and shenanigans.*

we mix our hidden liquor with Coke and 7-Up, laugh
and wonder at this *relic*; aromas of ginger, star anise,
and fragrant plum

rely on 'history-class knowledge' of railway ties — see men at other
tables, creased faces, dark eyes hunched over, pondering us —
feelings pop like fizz

in my drink; so I head to the washroom, take a wrong turn,
suddenly looking down into a smoke-filled nook
where several men sit
stilled;

over

the slouch of history
bending their backs —
silence
but
for the
tick
of
mahjong
tiles —
they all
turn to stare

apologetic, I return to the restaurant bursting
with patrons and piles of steaming food heaped on hot plates —
we devour ours like ravenous scavengers

pay the bargain bill; waft back onto the street
where apparitions from the past still wander the night air.
make our way beyond the abandoned

Shaw Theatre (ahead of its time, even back then) and
further up the street, cross the intersection out of
Chinatown to Gastown's Blarney Stone

and a line where midnight revelers wait for their turn at a table
in Vancouver's hustling night life. later the moon sighs
as we board our way out of the city port for shores
to the North. a horn sounds

and in the ship's wake thousands of ghosts hover —
listening for the dollar-a-day clank of the last spike,
straight through to the heart of Chinatown

rivaled only by the dragon's roar.

Under Glass
MorningStar Leon

The place was sold intact, with its furniture, tools, dishes, boat.
She'd taken the clothes out — her stepmother's,
furred with seven years' dust, went to the dump;
her father's, newer, to the men's shelter.
The glass-topped pine box with the stretched-straight-out
snake skeleton her stepmother had found,
and the pictures on the walls and tables —
mostly of the dogs and the one cat — and the albums,
where she did not find the one picture she wanted,
all this thrown out.

She thought then it might be in the boathouse.
The boat bays were empty. The Chris Craft long sold.
Her father's knees could no longer bend enough to get in and out.
She could see the Tin Fish tied to the dock through the cobwebs
that draped the window over the workbench.

Resting on the rafters, the canoe, its paddles, a toboggan.
Under the window, a cluster of dead shadflies, like crumpled tissue
    paper.
Lured by light they'd battered themselves to death against the
    window
A glass-front case on the wall protected the trout flies
he'd wrapped and woven when she was little.
Tools — hammers, corded drill, combination wrench set,
channel-lock pliers and vise grips, screwdrivers,
a chainsaw so long unused it would no longer start.

And a scissor. Is that what you call it?
One half of a broken pair? The other lost
or thrown out. Heaven knows what he'd used it for.
Cutting bait, maybe?

over

Half-a-dozen forty year-old snapshots
curling, tacked to the wall: the one
of her father, nose to nose in the river with the German Shepherd
they'd had when she was in high school.
Two or three of boats,
with or without fishermen; and the prize:
Her brother,
freckled, 11 years old, holding up a foot-long
grass pickerel. That's about as big as a grass pickerel gets
and as happy as he got in his life.

She felt some live wriggling in her gorge
like a worm or a minnow on a hook, trolled by the thing
that had trolled for her father, trapped him
in hopelessness and helplessness and bottles of Scotch.
It seemed to come with her brother's epilepsy
and dyslexia, his failures in school and juvie jail
and life. His only son. Not the son he'd wanted.
Not a son you could grow old with,
still fishing, handing you in and out of the boat
when your knees didn't work any more.

That fearsome, luring thing,
with its underslung jaw and scything teeth like Northern Pike,
took her brother. He hung himself,
from one of those rafters. And the old man,
half of a broken pair,
the other lost, his heart torn out,
sank and sank and sank
into the bottom of his bottles,
battered himself to death against them.

A Tender Attention
Chantelle Spicer

Rita reads a poem
and the land lifts its many voices alongside[1]

let me be free-free-free
    chickadee-dee-dee
nourishment can come in small bites
    blackberry begin to set
cleanse, wish, sense
    water runs joyfully over the rocks
unfurl yourself
    sword fern rises and opens
sssshhhhh
    a thousand, a thousand, a thousand leaves

your body can be a home
    cedar spreads her branches
glow where the sun touches you
    spring leaves of salmonberry carrying light
you change in relation
    stones along the creek bed transform

a symphony of poems.

---

1   Sitting, watching, and listening is a teaching I was gifted by Qwulshemut Ray Peter of Quw'utsun. As a Mi'kmaq and Jewish woman who has been forcibly displaced from my own teachings, these are gifts of this land and host nations that I cherish deeply. Though they are not my teachings, they are important teachings that are a part of learning how to be a good guest on these lands.

Big Fish Pink Salmon
Angie Conrad

Sunset drew my eyes high above the houses to Big Fish.
The washboard of grey scales in the west
   wrapped around the salmon-bodied sky.
      The biggest fish I ever saw.
         Could have fed all of Turtle Island.

Eight thousand gallons of chlorinated water
   held tight in a circle of plastic and metal
      perched on my assigned 0.08 acres of taxed city property.
My back against the wet
   and hungry eyes upwards.
Eight thousand gallons of stagnant water.
Chlorinated to keep it fresh.
Undrinkable.
And I thirst.

I watch the salmon as I begin my laps
One... two... three...
   Lap four and the salmon is strong

The wind speaks to the east pushing the colours out of shape
   Lap five... scales stretch

Lap six... grey and pink swirl together
   Cotton candy!
      And no more salmon in the sky
      and none in the stream

But I bought one at Superstore.
It was in its own tin can with a picture and words
   to tell me its name.

Lap seven…
                    The sky is changing faster than I can swim

33 laps to go.
The wind is stronger and faster than my rhythmic limbs.
        Big Fish torn apart
                Not sharing
                        Leaving my Spirit and stomach empty
I close my eyes
The sound clipped to my ears drowns out the death in the sky
39… 40…

Dripping wet and city clean, the water droplets from my hair
    bathe my kitchen floor.
The can opener tears the metal to release "Pink Salmon."

Firefly in a Jar
George Connell

One child at the sitter's and one more on the way
One more shot of coffee to get her through the day
No-one to help her make it through. He left her long ago
And every night she wished she had the power to say no

It wasn't meant to be this way. She should have been a star
A twinkle in the firmament, a firefly in a jar
She should have left this one-horse town while she still had the chance
But vows of mediocrity kept her from the dance

Now she tends the checkout in the village grocery store
Years fly by like windswept skies. She wanted so much more
One more night at home alone before the television
Celebrities reminding her each night what could have been

It wasn't meant to be this way. She should have been a star
A twinkle in the firmament, a firefly in a jar
She should have left this one-horse town while she still had the chance
But vows of mediocrity kept her in a trance

The cats are fed, the dishes washed, the laundry put away
She gazes through a magazine to dream of holidays
She shuts the door, turns out the lights, the key turns in the latch
Tomorrow is another day and she has dreams to catch

But she could have been somebody, she could have been a star
A twinkle in the firmament, a firefly in the jar

what Mama says
Leah Bobet

don't make my mistakes

my mistakes are mine

I only made them

to take them away

from you.

First Prize
Daniela Elza

Daniela Elza lived on three continents before immigrating to Canada in 1999. Her latest poetry collections are *the broken boat* (2020) and *slow erosions* (2020). Her work has won numerous contests and has been nominated for the Pushcart Prize and Best of the Net Anthology multiple times. She placed second in the 2022 Ken Belford Poetry Prize for Social Justice. She is a founding member of the Place Mattering Matters Collective and advocates for affordable housing in her community in Vancouver, located on the unceded territories of the xʷməθkʷəy̓əm (Musqueam), Sḵwx̱wú7mesh (Squamish), and səlilwətaɬ (Tsleil-Waututh) Nations.

PHOTO: Lynne Woodley

Second Prize
Cristy Watson

Cristy Watson currently creates on the lands of the Tsuu T'ina and is an award-winning author of eight novels for middle-grade and YA readers (Orca Book Publishers and Formac/Lorimer), as well as having her poetry included in anthologies such as: *Worth More Standing* (Caitlin Press), *Contemporary Verse 2*, and *The Poetry Marathon Anthology* (2017–present). She won HM in the first Coffee Shop Author Contest (sponsor, Oolichan Press) and has volunteered for over a decade at the Surrey International Writers Conference and, recently, with the BC Federation of Writers. Prior to the pandemic, she hosted an open mic in Surrey, BC.

DOWNTOWN EASTSIDE PRIZE
Gilles Cyrenne

Gilles Cyrenne lives on the ancestral unceded territory of the Squamish, Musqueam, and Tsleil-Waututh people. He coordinates the Downtown Eastside Writers Collective, serves as President of the Carnegie Community Centre Association, and is a mentor for the UBC Hum Writing 101 Program and for the UBC Science 101 Program which provide a series of free lectures for DTES and Downtown Southside residents. He has published one book of poetry and is working on a second.

FORTUNA'S CHOICE
MorningStar Leon

I attend and lead Zoom meetings for several international organizations. I have joined ceremonies for the Missing Children of Residential Schools and written letters to politicians and religious leaders requesting reparations. I am proud to live on the traditional lands of the Kwanlin Dun First Nation.

HONOURABLE MENTION
Chantelle Spicer

Weaving together poetics, land-based teachings, research, and self-reflective practices, Chantelle Spicer is doing the hard work of reconnecting to their own teachings and family who, due to anti-Semitism and colonialism, they have been disconnected from. While not writing, she is a part of many social movements at the intersections of Indigenous rights, climate justice, and abolition. These lands of "Vancouver" that she works on should be under jurisdiction of xʷməθkʷəy̓əm, Səlílwətaʔ, and Skwxwú7mesh nations but, due to structures of oppression that target Indigenous women and two-spirit people, are illegally claimed by Vancouver and Canada.

HONOURABLE MENTION
Angie Conrad

Oki! I acknowledge I am on the traditional territory of the Kainai Nation, the Piikani Nation, and the Siksika Nation in Southern Alberta as well as the Blackfeet Tribe of Northern Montana.

I live with my husband part-time on Salt Spring Island and part-time on the Alberta prairies. Our family has two homes. I love helping people in finding their ancestors and living relatives.

HONOURABLE MENTION
George Connell

I live on Shishalh land on the Sunshine Coast. Of the many things I do, one is to offer a 500 dollar award every year to a high school graduate who shows interest in/ proclivity towards the Arts.

HONOURABLE MENTION
Leah Bobet

My poetry has most recently appeared in *Prairie Fire*, *Canthius*, and *Reckoning: creative writing on environmental justice*'s special reproductive rights issue; it's forthcoming in *Strange Horizons*. My most recent novel, *An Inheritance of Ashes* (Scholastic Canada/ Clarion Books US), received the Aurora, Sunburst, and Copper Cylinder awards in 2016. I live in the traditional territory of the Mississaugas of the Credit, Anishnabeg, Chippewa, Haudenosaunee, and Wendat peoples. In my neighbourhood, I help organize a mutual aid network to get hot home-cooked meals, period supplies, and warm clothes to neighbours who need support, in encampments or outside them.

Judges' Statement

This year's writers were so exceptional that as a jury we found it difficult to come to a conclusion as to how to rank the poems and did multiple revisions to our placements before coming to a final decision. These discussions were lively, as each of us brought a unique perspective towards understanding the nature of poetry.

The work showcased diverse poetic forms and the subjects at times highlighted the direct lived experiences of the writers, while others experimented with displacement, nature, onomatopoeia, and structure of the line.

This is the 5th version of the Muriel's Journey Poetry Prize and one we were proud to play a role in continuing. We look forward to seeing what the future holds for this wonderful contest in honour of poet and social justice activist, Muriel Marjorie.

CANDIE TANAKA is a multiracial trans writer, artist, librarian, and graduate of The Writer's Studio program at Simon Fraser University. Their first YA book, *Baby Drag Queen*, was published with Orca Books in April 2023. They've also published work in *Resonance: Essays on the Craft of Life and Writing* with Anvil Press and *This Will Only Take A Minute: Canadian Flash Fiction* with Guernica Editions. Learn more at candietanaka.com.

Writer and editor HEIDI GRECO's body of work consists mostly of poetry. Her most recent book, *Glorious Birds: A Celebratory Homage to Harold and Maude* (published by Anvil Press in 2021), served as a prose departure in that it celebrates one of her favourite films. While still writing (reviews, blogs, and poems), she continues to dedicate time to matters of environmental protection. She lives on territory of the Semiahmoo First Nation. Find more at heidigreco.ca.

ROSEMARY GEORGESON is a Coast Salish/Sahtu Dene artist, storyteller, and writer from Galiano Island. Born and raised in the commercial fishing industry, and with a background in the Culinary Arts, she was the Aboriginal Storyteller at the Vancouver Public Library and has worked as an artist and community liaison for Vancouver Moving Theatre and urban ink productions. She co-wrote *We're All In this Together* and *Storyweaving*.